WHO WILL STAND?

Blessings In **Boldness**

MARGIE SHADE NELSON

WESTBOW
PRESS®

A DIVISION OF THOMAS NELSON
& ZONDERVAN

WestBow Press books may be ordered through booksellers or by contacting:

WestBow Press
A Division of Thomas Nelson & Zondervan
1663 Liberty Drive
Bloomington, IN 47403
www.westbowpress.com
844-714-3454

ISBN: 979-8-3850-2016-4 (sc)
ISBN: 979-8-3850-2017-1 (e)

Library of Congress Control Number: 2024904140

Print information available on the last page.

WestBow Press rev. date: 03/05/2024

Dedicated to those who have and will decide to stand.
Who will stand for what is right?
Be a voice, be a light
Someone unafraid to fight
For what they know is true
Could that one be you?
-MSN

Contents

Who Will Stand?

Spiritual warfare throughout the land
Broken vessels on every hand
The world is sinking in the sand
The question is, who will stand?
Who will stand for what is right?
Be a voice, be a light
Someone unafraid to fight
For what they know is true.
Could that one be you?
Who on earth in God's creation
Can speak the truth, lead the nation?
And do it without hesitation
Because it must be done.
Could you be the one?
Are we living just to live?
Or are we helping one another?
Are we preaching the True Gospel?
Or are we cheating our brother?
It's time we bring truth to our fellow man
In a world that keeps bowing
I ask who will stand?

Wherefore take unto you the whole armour of God,
that ye may be able to withstand in the evil day, and
having done all, to stand. Ephesians 6:13 KJV

Blessings In Boldness

There are blessings in boldness
The world needs to know
And a faith that will lead you, wherever you go
Blessings and boldness go hand in hand
If you're going to be bold, you must take a stand
There are blessings in boldness
The world needs to show
That when you step out
Your faith will grow
When you step out and follow God's plan
Your blessings and boldness will go hand in hand
Step out in boldness, let your light shine
Don't wait til tomorrow
Now is the time.

Be on your guard; stand firm in the faith; be
courageous; be strong. Do everything in love.
1 Corinthians 16:13-14 NIV

What Are We Waiting For?

No time to waste
We must embrace
This moment to stand tall
We must aim for the masses
If we aim at all
This world is in dire need
Of what we have to give
In order to succeed
We must learn to live
Life is but a vapor
It's here then gone away
Don't wait till tomorrow
Do your best today
God gives ample time
To fulfill His assignment
His grace is sufficient
In helping us find it
So let us not grow weary
Or faint along the way
Nor put off for tomorrow
What we can do today
Live a life of value
Make it count my friend
Live as God intended
Be salt and light to men.

"He that observeth the wind shall not sow; and he
that regardeth the clouds shall not reap."
Ecclesiastes 11:4 KJV

Speak Truth

A broken heart
A contrite spirit
A changed mind
For those who hear it
Once bound
Now free
Headed for eternity
Speak truth, no lies
Never should we compromise
Sins forgiven
No disguise
The time has come for us to rise.

Wherefore putting away lying, speak every
man truth with his neighbor:
for we are members one of another. Ephesians 4:25 KJV

A Corrupt World

This world's corrupt and rightly so
We've given way for sin to grow
We've broken Your laws in families and schools
We've turned from the truth
And made our own rules
We've chosen to do what we think is right
By walking in darkness and shunning the Light
Homosexuality and transgender sins
We now accept because they're family and friends
There's much to be said of this world today
Our morals and values have slipped away
This world's corrupt and rightly so
All because we've let You go
And yes, You've made it very clear on what we need to do
That's turn from our wicked ways
Repent and turn to You.

If My people who are called by My name will humble
themselves, and pray and seek My face,
and turn from their wicked ways, then I will hear from
heaven, and will forgive their sin and heal their land.
2 Chronicles 7:14 NKJV

God's Rainbow

Never use God's rainbow
To represent your sin
God's rainbow is a symbol
Of what won't be again
Its meaning and its purpose
We mustn't put aside
To stand for what is sinful
Like homosexual pride
Its meaning and its purpose
Forever stays the same
That the earth will end with fire
And never again with rain.

I set my rainbow in the cloud, and it shall be for the sign of the covenant between Me and the earth. Genesis 9:13 NKJV

Stand Strong

For those of you who've overcome
Be not afraid stand strong
Someone needs to hear your story
For their good and God's glory
Let's not ignore what we see
Faces of captivity
Right before our very eyes
Acts of sin are on the rise
You've come through unashamed
Now help someone to do the same
Your efforts will not be in vain
This I know is true
That God can also rescue them
Like He rescued you.

Wherefore take unto you the whole armour of
God, that ye may be able to withstand
in the evil day, and having done all, to stand. Ephesians 6:13 KJV

It's Time

Rise up, Step out
It's time to take a stand
It's time to show the world
That we love God more than man
It's time to go to war
This time our choice
May God be our hands and feet
May He be our voice
Walk straight, don't sway
Look ahead, not away
May we never fail to fight
For what we know is true and right
And in the darkness be a light
As we simply stand.

But I will sing of thy power; Yea, I will sing
aloud of thy mercy in the morning;
For thou hast been my defense and refuge in
the day of my trouble. Psalm 59:16 KJV

Acknowledge God

If every day were sunny
We wouldn't need light
If every day were battle free
We wouldn't need to fight
If every problem that we face
We could understand
We'd have no need for God
Our trust would be in man
We must stay focused
And never lose sight
That Jesus is our sustenance
He is the Light
So let us not grow weary
And give up on a whim
Though life gets dark and dreary
Let's place our trust in Him.

Trust in the LORD with all thine heart; and lean
not unto thine own understanding.
In all thy ways acknowledge Him, and he shall direct thy path.
Proverbs 3:5-6 KJV

A Grateful Heart

Father keep me near the cross
Each and everyday
I am here to worship You
In every single way
I will raise the banner
As high as it will go
And give You all the glory
My God I've come to know
I will serve the world
The gifts you've given me
I'll reach beyond the masses
To help set others free
And if tomorrow comes
I'll do it all again
Lord, I thank You for the gift
To touch the hearts of men.

And whatever you do, whether in word or deed,
do it all in the name of the Lord Jesus,
giving thanks to God the Father through him Colossians 3:17 NIV

Father Knows Best

I'm here on a mission
And powerfully led
To walk in the Spirit
As Jesus said
To live out my calling
Given at birth
To crush satan's head
While here on the earth
Wherever I go
I will let my light shine
For those in front
And those behind
As God's grace and mercy
Continues to bless
I will walk in His Truth
Because Father knows best.

Casting all your care upon Him, for He
cares for you. I Peter 5:7 KJV

Better Days Ahead

Heavenly Father it's been a rough day
I know you understand
For nothing rough would come my way
If it weren't in Your plan
You always place me back on track
When my life derails
Your truth endures forever
And Your mercy never fails
Thank You for showing me
How lost my life would be
If You hadn't sent Your Son
To earth to die for me
Because You made it possible
For sins to be forgiven
Every day's a new day
And every day worth living.

But as it is written, Eye hath not seen, nor ear
heard, neither have entered into the heart
of man, the things which God hath prepared for
them that love him. I Corinthians 2:9 NIV

Make Me Better

Father make me better
Than I've ever been
Forgiving those who hurt me
And repenting for my sins
To pray in the good times
And not just in the bad
To praise You when I'm happy
And even when I'm sad
Father make me better
The best that I can be
As we walk together
Make me more like Thee.

Have nothing to do with godless myths
and old wives' tales; rather,
train yourself to be godly. I Timothy 4:7 NIV

We Can't Shock God

There's nothing I can do
That will shock You
You knew what my life would bring
That is why You died for me
That is why You came
I must never take for granted
The love You have for me
Nor ever take credit
For what I've come to be
May the gifts You've given me
Remain upon display
And used as an instrument
To lead the world Your way.

You know when I sit and when I rise; you perceive my thoughts
from afar. You discern my going out and my lying down;
you are familiar with all my ways. Psalm 139: 2-3 NIV

Faith That Grows

With God as my Song
I've learned to be strong
My world is brighter
My burdens lighter
My eyes are open
My walk is straight
I've learned that good things
Come when I wait
He's healed my heart
He's answered my prayer
He's done so much
I can't help but share
I'll make it plain
For the world to know
My faith was once small
But God helped it grow.

And the apostles said unto the Lord,
Increase our faith. Luke 17:5 KJV

Embrace Your Dreams

Take note of your dreams
And chase them
Let no one erase them
They were your's from the start
When God placed in your heart
The desire for you to embrace them.

Delight thyself also in the LORD; and he shall give thee
the desires of thine heart. Psalm 37:4 KJV

We Don't Weep Alone

The Lord is touched by your weaknesses
Your painful yearning heart
By the struggles that you face
By your cries in the dark
He's touched by your infirmities
And will from day to day
Remind you, He's with you
And listens when you pray
Have joy in knowing
That you are His own
That when you weep
You don't weep alone
He wipes every tear
Away from your face
Extending His love
Mercy and Grace.

Thou tellest my wanderings: put thou my tears into thy
bottle: are they not in thy book? Psalm 56:8 KJV

17

Hear Me Lord

Father stop my heart from racing
Ease my mind
Stop my feet from pacing
You alone can clean my mess
Forgive my sins as I confess
Comfort me and give me rest
As only You can do
Father see me through
You alone can tame the races
Remove the mask from people's faces
Reveal our scars in hidden places
Then bring us to our knees
Oh, Father help us please!
You alone can dry our tears
Remove our doubts
Diminish fears
Prepare us for the coming years
As only You can do
I place my trust in You.

I love the LORD, for he heard my voice, he heard my cry for mercy. Because he turned his ear to me. I will call on him as long as I live. Psalm 116:1-2 NIV

The Holy Ghost

Though fires rage
You're not alone
God is with you
You're His own
If on water
You should sink
Know He's closer
Than you think
He's right there
To rescue you
To pull you out
And help you through
If a storm should wreck your boat
Do not fear, in God there's hope
He's Water for the fire
And Peace in the storm
He fixes what is broken
And mends what is torn
Forever present when needed most
Is our Comforter and Helper
The Holy Ghost.

And I will pray the Father, and he shall give you another
Comforter, that he may abide with you forever; John 14:16 KJV

In Step with the Spirit

He's no shorter than His Word
And sticks closer than a brother
When you seek Him you will find Him
A love like no other
In your toiling
He'll relieve you
Your path He'll make straight
When He doesn't answer quickly
He'll teach you to wait
You may not get a miracle
Everywhere you go
But the ones you'll encounter
Will surely help you grow
Keep step with the Spirit
Let Him lead the way
Live your life intentionally
Each and every day.

If we live by the Spirit, Let us also keep in step
with the Spirit. Galatians 5:25 ESV

Make It Count

— ❧ —

Enjoy the moment while it's here
Don't take life for granted dear
Say the words you need to say
Before the moment slips away
Share the love you have inside
And let the Lord be glorified.

Teach us to number our days, that we may gain
a heart of wisdom. Psalm 90:12 NIV

Take No Thought/TNT

Take no thought
I heard Him say
I've walked the path
I've paved the way
I'm the Bread of Life indeed
When you have Me
I'm all you need
To walk this journey unafraid
For now the price is fully paid
Because of you I came to earth
To demonstrate how much you're worth
So take no thought about today
Of food or drink or clothes I say
For I'm the Bread of Life indeed
And will supply your every need.

But seek ye first the kingdom of God, and His righteousness and all these things shall be added unto you. Matthew 6:33 KJV

Notice

For every no, there's a yes
For every better, there's a best
For every trial, there's a test
For in Christ we're blessed.
It's in Him we find rest for our soul.

God's Already There

Wherever God goes
He's already there
Wherever I am
He's already here
Wherever I've been
He's there too
And wherever you are
He's there with you.

Can any hide himself in secret places that I
shall not see him? saith the LORD.
Do not I fill heaven and earth? saith the LORD. Jeremiah 23:24 KJV

Forever Worship

When we get to heaven
We'll all be the same
Completely engulfed with the love of our King
In total surrender
We'll bow at His feet
And partake of the table
With plenty to eat
We'll rest in His presence
Full of delight
Where it's always day
And never night
No need for contention
No need to fight
For we'll all be in sync
As we worship the Light.

I will exalt you, my God the King; I will praise
your name for ever and ever.
Every day I will praise you and extol your name
forever and ever. Psalm 145:1-2 NIV

Sin is Sin

There is no sin great or small
If you're guilty of one
Then you're guilty of all.

For whoever keeps the whole law but fails in one point
has become accountable for all of it. James 2:10 ESV

God Is Love

God is love, but there are things He hates
Immorality gets Him irate
And though we're loved
From beginning to end
There's a price to pay
For habitual sin
So don't take lightly the things you do
Nor live your life just for you
For in the end a price will be paid
And you will be judged
By the choices you've made.

I will instruct you and teach you in the way you should go;
I will counsel you with my loving eye on you. Psalm 32:8 NIV

A Fresh Start

A new chapter starts
An old chapter ends
A story is finished
A new one begins
God has forgiven
They're no longer your sins
Take hold of His grace
And start over again.

"Forget the former things, do not dwell on the past.
See, I am doing a new thing!" Now it springs up; do
you not perceive it? I am making a way in the wilderness
and streams in the wasteland. Isaiah 43:18-19 NIV

Yahweh

Your Word
Your Will
Your Way
Today and everyday Yahweh!

I am Yahweh, that is My name; I will not give My
glory to another, or My praise to Idols.
Isaiah 42:8 CSB

Everyday You're Loved

Every day is a new day, and everyday you're loved!

The steadfast love of the Lord never ceases; His mercies never come to an end; they are new every morning; great is your faithfulness. Lamentations 3:22-23 ESV

My Anchor

We all need an Anchor
To help keep us grounded
A symbol of love
With power around it
My Anchor is the Lord.

This hope is a strong and trustworthy anchor
for our souls. It leads us through the curtain into
God's inner sanctuary. Hebrews 6:19 NLT

Spiritual Hugs

Some hugs are weak and others strong
Some are short and some are long
But spiritual hugs of great endeavor
Embrace the heart and last forever.

Jesus Christ Is King

Jesus Christ is King
He's Lord of everything
There's nothing we can do
To change His Holy name
There's nothing we can do
To equal what He's done
No my friend, He never sinned
And He's the only One
A crown of thorns pierced His head
Blood ran down His face
No my friend, He never sinned
But died to take our place
If ever you are burdened
Low and in despair
Remember He is risen
And has you in His care
Don't let sin defeat you
Don't let it bring you down
For where sin abounded,
Grace did much more abound.

And God is able to make all grace abound to you,
so that having all sufficiency in all things at all times,
you may abound in every good work. 2 Corinthians 9:8 (ESV)

Remember The Cross

Count your blessings day by day
And don't dismiss a thing
Remember why God sent His Son
And why we call Him King
Don't forget the blood He shed
While hanging on the cross
Nor the thorns upon His head
To represent the lost
Don't forget the stripes He took
That bore our every sin
Don't forget He died and rose
To never die again
He did it all for us
And did it without lack
He proved His love for us
Now we must love Him back.

And you must love the Lord your God with all your heart,
all your soul, all your mind, and all your strength;
Mark 12:30 NLT

The Lord Is My Anchor

The Lord is my Anchor
He steadies my boat
When I'm on water
He keeps me afloat
When I'm in the desert
He shades my skin
When I'm in a storm
He calms the wind
When I'm confused
He's peace within
When I repent
He forgives my sins
Then gives me a chance
To start over again
The Lord is my Anchor
And always will be
My Anchor on land
And my Anchor at sea.

This hope is a strong and trustworthy anchor for our souls.
It leads us through the curtain into God's
inner sanctuary. Hebrews 6:19 NLT

Forgiveness Opens Doors

The things that truly matter
Are the things that truly work
Like asking forgiveness
From someone you've hurt
It's when you surrender
And let the Lord in
That your heart is changed
From deep down within
He'll open your eyes
And show you your wrongs
That your days have been numbered
And your journey's not long
May the evil that holds you
Hold you no more
And may your heart find forgiveness
To open the door.

"Be kind and compassionate to one another, forgiving each other, just as in Christ God forgave you." NIV Ephesians 4:32

Forgiveness Is Key

Forgiveness is key
This we must do
You must forgive others
Like God forgives you
It matters not who started the fight
Who was wrong or who was right
Unforgiveness feeds pain
And you must set it free
The choice is yours
To unlock the doors
And forgiveness is the key.

"Be kind and compassionate to one another, forgiving each other,
just as in Christ God forgave you." NIV Ephesians 4:32

Obedience and Faith

Obedience is key and
faith is the door that God answers.

Whoever gives heed to instruction prospers, and
blessed is the one who trusts in the LORD.
Proverbs 16:20 NIV

The God I Know

Ask forgiveness while you can
Seek His face that's His command
Knock and He will let you in
That's the God I know.

"Ask and it will be given to you; seek and you will
find; knock and the door will be opened to you. For
everyone who ask receives; the one who seeks finds;
and the one who knocks, the door will be opened.
Matthew 7:7-12 NIV

I Keep Holding On

Lord, I'm lost without You
I need You everyday
I can't live life without You
Protect and lead the way
Without You I'd be empty
My life would be a mess
Thank You for reminding me
Of how much I am blessed
Even when I'm weak
I can say I'm strong
It's Your love for me
That keeps me holding on.

For I the Lord thy God will hold thy right hand, saying unto thee,
Fear not; I will help thee. Isaiah 41:13 KJV

Fix Your Eyes On Jesus

Fix your eyes on Jesus
Let nothing blind your view
Focus on His goodness
And all He's done for you
Recall how He forgave you
For your ruthless sins
That even though you hurt Him
He still calls you friend
Fix your eyes on Jesus
There's nothing greater still
Then the King of Glory
Who died and rose for real!

Looking unto Jesus the author and finisher of our
faith; who for the joy that was set before
Him endured the cross, despising the shame, and is set down
at the right hand of the throne of God. Hebrews 12:2 KJV

We're Only Passing Through

When storm clouds invade the sky
When billows roll and seagulls cry
When we can't see eye to eye
And know not what to do
Say a prayer and be aware
We're only passing through
When enemies are all around
And friends are nowhere to be found
When there are less ups than downs
And you don't know what to do
Say a prayer and be aware
We're only passing through.
This world is not our home
God has a home for you
You see my friend
It's not the end
We're only passing through.

For we know that if the tent that is our earthly home
is destroyed, we have a building from God,
a house not made with hands, eternal in
the heavens. 2 Corinthians 5:1 ESV

My Friend Paul

A loyal servant
A trusted friend
One on whom you could depend
Seventy years went by fast
The love
The joy
The jokes
The laughs
I'm pleased to say he knew the Lord
And lived his life that way
Loving others as himself
And taking time to pray
Somewhere in the darkness
He met the Lord that night
The Father's hands engulfed him
And brought him to the Light
No, I'm not bitter
That he's passed away
For I'm a firm believer that
We'll meet again someday.

Blessed are those who mourn, for they will
be comforted. Matthew 5:4 NIV

It's Okay

It's okay to feel tired
It's okay to need rest
It's okay to change course
It's okay to confess
It's okay to choose peace
Of which no man can give
It's okay to go out on a journey well lived
So don't be ashamed, that it's come down to this
For a life well lived, will surely be missed
You came out with a cry
Now return with a smile
Eternity's yours
You're forever God's child.

Psalm 23:4 KJV
Yea, though I walk through the valley of the
shadow of death, I will fear no evil:
for thou art with me, Thy rod and thy staff they comfort me.

Woulda, Shoulda, Coulda

I woulda, shoulda, coulda
Given of my time
Lent a listening ear
To hear what's on your mind
Called you on the phone
Just to hear your voice
All of this I should have done
Because I had a choice
I woulda, shoulda, coulda
Sought to make it right
Our little spats and quarrels
Which kept me up at night
When I saw you as a burden
And failed to put you first
I woulda, shoulda, coulda
Helped you see your worth
Now it's come to this
Time has ticked away
All that would have mattered
Remains in yesterday
Please forgive my selfishness
For all I didn't do
I woulda, shoulda, coulda
Shown a deeper love for you.

Do not boast about tomorrow, for you do not
know what a day may bring forth.
Do what you need to do today. Proverbs 27:1 NIV

Nursing Home Blues/One Voice

Would someone hear my humble plea
I need someone to rescue me
Would someone hear my tired voice
They brought me here
I had no choice
For if I had refused to go
They would have brought me still you know
And if I didn't want to stay
They would have left me anyway
I can't do what I used to do
Like walk, run or tie my shoe
People know, because they see
So they walk all over me
I lose control and wet the bed
I now need help to prop my head
They pressure me to make me stand
My cup it trembles in my hand
They treat me bad, but won't say why
They sometimes make me want to cry
Please Lord, hear my humble plea
And send someone to rescue me.

Even to your old age and gray hairs I am
he, I am he who will sustain you.
I have made you and I will carry you; I will sustain
you and I will rescue you. Isaiah 46:4 NIV

Nine Eleven

People left home
Went to their jobs
Entered the towers
With the usual mobs
Good morning and hello
Echoed the scene
As they prepared for their daily routine
Some arrived early and others on time
With visions of loved ones still on their mind
Some thought of the fight they had early on
That was never resolved before leaving that morn
Some reluctantly sat at their desk
With thoughts of the future and how they'd invest
Some minds were fully on family and friends
While some were engrossed in their personal sins
Suddenly evil reared it's ugly head
Planes crashed the towers now thousands are dead
Phone calls were made to help ease the sorrow
Realizing for them there would be no tomorrow
Tragedy struck on the eleventh of September
A day that our nation will always remember.

Boast not thyself of tomorrow for thou knowest not
what a day may bring forth. Proverbs 27:1 KJV

Katie

My heart is filled with joy
To know that you will be
The wife of my son
And daughter-in-law to me
A blessing in the making
A sister-in-law and friend
No longer on the outside
You've now been ushered in
Today's your bridal shower
And I'm wishing you the best
May your life be filled with
Love, joy, peace and happiness.

I'd Shine For You

If I were the sun
On a cloudy day
I'd shine for you
With you I'd stay
If I were the moon
On your darkest night
I'd shine for you with all my might
If I were a drink to pour in your cup
I wouldn't do half
I'd fill it up
It's truly an honor to share in your life
The wonderful blessings of being your wife.

"For this reason, a man will leave his father
and mother and be united to his wife,
and the two will become one flesh." Ephesians 5:31 NIV

Happy Mother's Day

Every day is Mother's Day, and everyday you're loved!
Happy Mother's Day!

May your father and mother rejoice; may she who
gave you birth be joyful! Proverbs 23:25 NIV

Happy Father's Day

————— ❧❧❧ —————

Every day is Father's Day, and everyday you're loved!
Happy Father's Day!

May your father and mother rejoice; may she who
gave you birth be joyful! Proverbs 23:25 NIV

Happy 90th Birthday!

Another year has come and gone
And you are very blessed
The Lord has brought you safe thus far
Through many trials and tests
The Lord has allowed you
To walk within His grace
And we have come to celebrate
Your birthday in this place
May today remind you
That we truly care
That you're truly loved
That God answers prayer
Today's your special day
It's your time to shine
To say hello to ninety
And goodbye to eighty-nine.

This is the day which the LORD hath made; we will
rejoice and be glad in it. Psalms 118:24 KJV

Happy 100th Birthday Dad!

Happy birthday Dad to you
For ninety-nine and a half won't do
You said it loud
You made it clear
And now you've reached your hundredth year
God has brought you safe thus far
Into the man we know you are
Much accomplished
Much achieved
You've given much
Now receive
This celebration is for you
For all you've done
And for all you do
You are blessed and you are strong
Which brings me to your favorite song
You truly are a living testimony
Today's your day to shine
You've outlived ninety-nine
Let's enjoy this special time together.

This is the day which the LORD hath made; we will
rejoice and be glad in it. Psalms 118:24 KJV

Printed in the United States
by Baker & Taylor Publisher Services